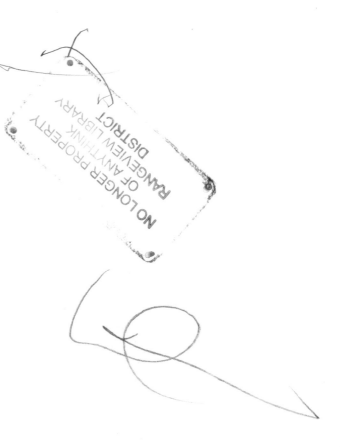

# LEARN TO DRAW
# *Adventurous*
# *Princesses*

This library edition published in 2020 by Walter Foster Jr.,
an imprint of The Quarto Group
26391 Crown Valley Parkway, Suite 220
Mission Viejo, CA 92691, USA.

Distributed in the United States and Canada by
Lerner Publisher Services
241 First Avenue North
Minneapolis, MN 55401 U.S.A.
www.lernerbooks.com

First Library Edition

Library of Congress Cataloging-in-Publication Data

Title: Disney princess : learn to draw adventurous princesses.
Other titles: Disney princess (Walter Foster Jr. (Firm))
Description: First library edition. | Mission Viejo, CA : Walter Foster Jr.,
    an imprint of The Quarto Group, 2020. | Audience: Ages: 6+. Audience:
    Grades: 4-6.
Identifiers: LCCN 2019017158 | ISBN 9781600588303 (hardcover)
Subjects: LCSH: Princesses in art--Juvenile literature. | Disney characters
    in art--Juvenile literature. | Drawing--Technique--Juvenile literature.
Classification: LCC NC825.P75 D57 2020 | DDC 741.5/973--dc23 LC record
available at https://lccn.loc.gov/2019017158

Printed in USA
9 8 7 6 5 4 3 2 1

Disney
PRINCESS

# LEARN TO DRAW
## Adventurous
### Princesses

# Table of Contents

# How to Use This Book

Just follow these simple steps, and you'll be amazed
at how fun and easy drawing can be!

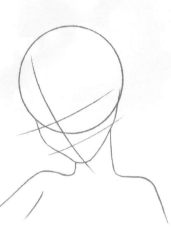

 **1** Draw the basic shape of the character; then add simple guidelines to help you place the features.

 **2** Each new step is shown in blue. Simply follow the blue lines to add the details.

 **3** Erase any lines you don't want to keep.

 **4** Use crayons, markers, colored pencils, or paints to add color.

# Disney

# POCAHONTAS

# Pocahontas

When the free-spirited and curious Pocahontas meets the English settler John Smith, they learn about each other's worlds. She bravely throws herself in front of him to prevent her father, Chief Powhatan, from executing him. Her selfless cry for peace stops a war between the settlers and her tribe.

4

5

# Meeko

The always-hungry Meeko is Pocahontas' raccoon friend. He and a ruby-throated hummingbird named Flit are always by Pocahontas' side. It is because of Meeko's curiosity that Pocahontas and John Smith meet. He immediately takes a liking to John Smith because he gives him biscuits, but Flit is much less trusting of strangers.

# Mulan

Cutting off her hair and disguising herself as a man, Mulan sets off to join the army in her father's place. She shows incredible bravery in fighting against the Huns, and when she finally returns home, Mulan realizes that she has brought her family honor by being true to herself.

1

2

# Mushu

Mushu is a tiny but mighty dragon and guardian to the Fa family. He was demoted from guardian to gong ringer after some past mishaps (he allowed Fa Deng to lose his head), but after helping Mulan save China, his guardian status was reinstated.

# Tiana

Tiana dreams of opening her very own restaurant in New Orleans. She works multiple waitressing jobs, having no time for any sort of social life. It is only when she is accidentally turned into a frog that Tiana learns that love is as important as hard work.

Tiana has dimples on her cheeks

Nose is about same width as the distance between eyes

YES! large, rounder eyes

NO! too narrow

1

Head shape resembles an egg

2

Narrow wrists

**3**

Tiana's bayou wedding crown is made of petals and stamens of varying shapes and sizes

Full bottom lip

**4**

Nose is short
and round

Rounded chin

5

YES!
ears are
small and
rounded

NO!
too
pointy

# Tiana the Frog

Being green isn't easy! When Tiana is transformed into a frog, she's faced with brand new challenges: finding her way through the bayou, escaping from frog hunters, and catching flies with her long, sticky tongue! But even as a frog, Tiana proves that she's very capable and hardworking. Whether it's making a boat on which to float down the bayou or whipping up a batch of gumbo for her friends, Tiana can get things done.

Tiana's eyes are one eye's width apart

1

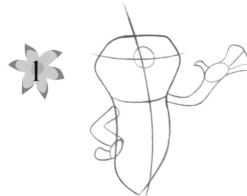

YES!
fingertips are wide

NO!
but not too wide

2

Second toe is the largest

3

4

5

Eyebrow

Full lashes

Eyelid

Disney

# Tangled

# Rapunzel

Rapunzel, locked away in a tower deep in the woods, has 70 feet of magical, golden hair. One day she escapes and begins the long journey back to the castle where she is reunited with her family and becomes the princess she was meant to be.

1

The "swoop" at the top of Rapunzel's hair is a distinguishing feature of her look

**2**

**3**

NO!

YES!

hair has volume
and thickness, even when
lying on
the floor

**4**

Rapunzel's hair has a lot of weight that forms simple shapes

**5**

6

# Pascal

Pascal is Rapunzel's best friend. The friendly chameleon has a way of understanding whatever Rapunzel is feeling—and he reflects it by changing color and expressions. She shares her innermost secrets with him, and she never has to worry that he will tell anyone!

1

Careful with the shape of the head

NO!     YES!

not like a
shark fin

a bit
rounded

2

**3**

**4**

Feet have 3 toes

**5**

Tail can unroll
to express emotion

# Merida

Headstrong and independent, Merida wants to do things her own way. She hates having to learn etiquette and behave like a proper lady. She would much rather spend her days in the woods, riding her horse, Angus, and practicing her archery.

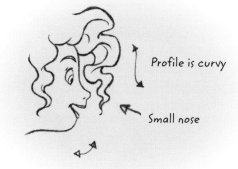

Profile is curvy

Small nose

1

2

3

For Merida's hair, use wild, squiggly lines

**4**

Merida's eyes

NO!    YES!

**5**

6

# Elinor the Bear

Elinor is transformed into a bear when she eats a cake that the Witch gave to Merida. Merida and Elinor the Bear embark on a journey to find the Witch to change Elinor back, and in the process, mother and daughter grow closer than ever.

1

2

**3**

NO!     not spaced
        too evenly

YES!    five claws
        grouped
        together

**4**

NO!          YES!

not          ears rounded
pointy

No cartoony eyes

5

6

52

# Moana

Now 16 years old and ready to become a master wayfinder, Moana is strong-willed and adventurous. She longs for the open ocean despite her father's demands that she stay within the reef.

Moana is about 5 ½ heads tall

1

2

3

4

5

Almond-shaped eyes,
with thick eyelashes
and eyebrows

Eyes are angled like this

6

YES! Moana's hands and feet are strong and rounded

NO! not thin and angular

7

8

# Pua

Pua is an adorable and gentle spotted pig who lives on Motunui with Moana. Moana saved Pua when she saw that he was the runt of the litter and wasn't getting enough food. Now Pua is fiercely loyal and always supportive of Moana.

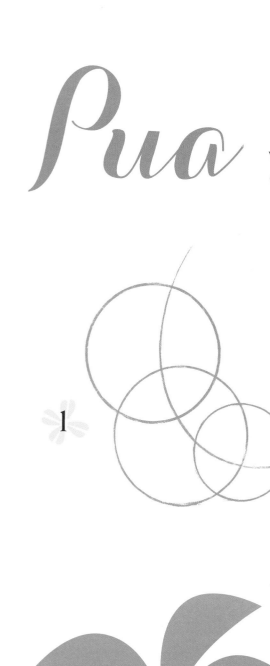

1

Pua is about 2 heads tall

2

3

4

5

6

7

Pua is ¹/₇ taller than Heihei

# Don't miss these other books by Walter Foster Jr.!

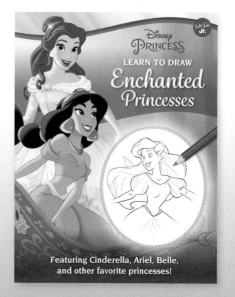

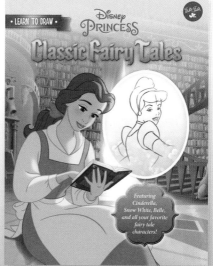

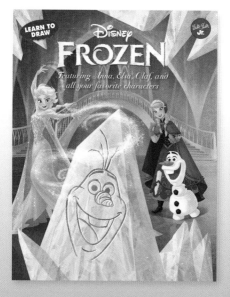

**Disney Princess:
Learn to Draw
Enchanted Princesses**
ISBN: 978-1-60058-831-0

**Learn to Draw Disney's
Classic Fairy Tales**
ISBN: 978-1-94287-547-5

**Learn to Draw Disney's
Frozen**
ISBN: 978-1-93958-164-8

Visit QuartoKnows.com for more
Learn to Draw Disney books.